Rhymes of Passion

Davy Edge

To David

Best wishes, always

x

First published in October 2024

ISBN:
978-1-0687104-0-7

Published by Off the Lip Publishing

www.davyedge.wordpress.com

Printed by: Rufford Printing Company
The Design Shed, Cedar Farm
Back Lane, Mawdesley, Ormskirk, L40 3SY

This book is dedicated to the
Inner Sanctum, as I call them –
my closest friends, who have
become family; who help and
support me in so many ways. I am
blessed to have them in my Life.
A huge 'Thank you' to Bill Evans -
graphic designer extraordinaire
and true gentleman, who put his
time, his hard work, and his
expertise into the physical
manifestations of all three
of my books.
I am eternally grateful to him.

© CYRANO DENN
A FABULOUS CREATION
© CYRANO DENN

PREFACE

Welcome to 'Rhymes of Passion';
poems of diversity,
nestling within the pages,
in this part of my trilogy.
Enjoy these sundry words and thoughts!
Let them set your spirit free!
May you find a form of serenity,
between the covers of book three!
May my bon mots bring a smile to your face,
and my musings make you think.
For the pen is more powerful than the sword,
when dipped in honest ink.
So enjoy this tertiary volume of words.
plumbed from the depths of my mind.
Kick off your shoes, and pull up a chair,
and let yourself unwind!.

FOREWORD

Friends now for over forty years, I was genuinely so pleased to write a few lines for this, the third part of Davy's trilogy of poems.

We first met in 1982 at the Liverpool Playhouse when we were both cast in the original production of Blood Brothers and have trod the boards together many times since then.

We've shared music, words, and laughter...it's a joy to sing with someone who knows what you're thinking!

I've watched first-hand the effect Davy has on an audience, whether in a large auditorium or in an intimate venue. A skilled musician and clever wordsmith, his work evokes laughter and tears. People listen!

His pen can be mightier than the sword or as soft as a blanket.

My partner in crime – a master of rhyme. His words bring pleasure, understanding, and hope. Enjoy them all.

Eithne Browne
July 2024

CONTENTS

CONTENTS

CONTENTS

A Special Occasion

She'd saved it for a "special occasion",
and kept it in a drawer,
still in its wrapping.
He found it when he was sorting through
her things,
after the funeral.
And the coat she'd never worn...
residing at the back of the wardrobe;
saved, for a "special occasion"
which never arrived.
He pondered that each new day
had been the "special occasion"
she had waited for.
Each day had been the important celebration.
He put on the tie she had bought him
for a "special occasion",
and walked out into the fresh morning air.

Too Much to Say

When somebody ruffles your feathers,
be a clever bird!
Don't be tempted to argue back.
Don't even proffer a word.
Treat it with the contempt it deserves,
and go about your day.
The trouble with some people is
that they have too much to say.
Keep your cool, and let the fool
ramble on and on.
It doesn't even matter
if they think that they have won.
What matters most is your inner peace,
so let them spout away!
Focus your mind on higher things,
and let the donkey bray!

A Life Well-Lived

To Live Life well, should be our aim -
To celebrate each day -
To learn about what makes us tick,
and not worry our time away -
To give of ourselves and not give in -
To love ourselves enough -
To focus our minds on higher things,
and not sweat the smaller stuff -
To be of generous heart and tongue -
To give praise wherever it's due -
To not be fazed when Life gets tough,
and to always see things through -
To be grateful for each morning,
and thankful at each eve -
To count our blessings, at the end of the day,
more blessings to receive.
For Life is an amazing journey.
Never think that it's not.
It is whatever you make of it -
so give it all you've got!!!

Year

January comes with ice and snow;
February's not much better!
March is when the cold winds blow.
April's even wetter!
May is when the flowers bloom
as the sun begins to shine.
Flaming June is gone too soon,
but July's looking fine!
August, we are hot and sweaty;
cottons and linens abound.
September, leaves fall like confetti,
and strew themselves around.
October brings the darker nights;
November's on the rise;
December's time for Christmas lights,
and eating too many mince pies!
So let us give each day our best -
For these are the days of our Lives!!!

Whiskey Abhor

It seems strange to single something out,
be it made from mash or from must;
but I have to share my experience,
before my bones become dust.
Beer is bad, and wine is worse,
but whiskey is out on its own.
I hope when you reach the end of my verse,
you'll drop it like a stone.
It may feel like it's warming,
when you wallop whiskey down;
but what it's doing is wasting you,
you whiskey-sodden clown!
It'll gnaw away at your self-esteem,
that dangerous, demonic drink.
It'll change your personality,
and send you over the brink.
It'll strip away your dignity,
your friends and family, too.
And when it's taken all you have,
it'll come back, then, for you.
It's never too late to reclaim your Life.
It's all down to the way you think!
So, take that bottle by its scrawny neck,
and pour it down the sink!

A Poet's Dream

O, that love presided over all!
Then would this weary globe happy on its
axis turn!
Each wandering soul would find its way home;
and broken spirits would contentment learn.
And I should write of nought but grace;
for sadness would be obsolete.
Smiles would be on every face,
on every rainy, city street.
Each tortured mind would find its peace.
Each tired body, its rest.
Each fear and worry would be washed away,
from every troubled breast.
And is it madness to fantasise so?
To hold such things in one's heart?
Then, mad as a hatter, I'll dream away;
and ply my fractur'd art.

Position Seventeen

It's not from the Kama Sutra,
or anything taboo.
Position seventeen, I am...
waiting in a queue.
There's uninspiring music
playing down my ear,
I'm expecting a voice from nowhere,
to come through, loud and clear.
"You're in position seventeen" she says.
My vigil has begun.
I wonder how long I'll be hanging on
before I reach number one.
I try to stay in the moment,
and focus my thoughts on my breath.
Perhaps I'll still be waiting,
when my eyelids have closed in death.
I ponder on eternity,
and what it must be like.
Will Hell be an eternal ride
on an exercise bike?
All of these things I think of, and more,
such as what Life itself must mean.
I'll have solved the problems of the World,
before I'm position sixteen...

A Saturday in the Seventies

You went to Burton's to buy your suit;
your shirt, and your tie as well.
If you saved up your cash,
you could go on the lash
in shoes that you bought from Ravel.
The collars were round; the music was sound;
the girls were as cute as could be.'
From Tom Hall's Tavern,
you'd go to The Cavern,
where you'd try to bunk in for free.
The Seventies were a special time
to anyone who was there.
You'd boogie on 'til Wonderland -
that place where you hadn't a care.
And when it came to five to two,
you'd smoothie on to the floor.
You and your mate would cast your fate
to the blondes dancing nearest the door.
"Fancy a dance?" "Do you fancy your chance
for the very last slowie of the night?"
You'd plenty of Dutch courage,
and the backing of Barry White.
Oh, the plight of the teenage heart!
It never fails to fall.
You thought you were John Travolta;
she said you weren't that tall.

And so you walked the long miles home,
with not a cab in sight.
smoking the last of your cigarettes,
and cursing Barry White.
Your flares were soaked at the bottoms,
your aftershave had long worn off.
You knew you'd wake in the morning
with a dry mouth and a cough.
Still! They were the days to Live!
To sing! To be young! To dance!
Yet, I would never wish them back
those days of sweet romance.
For now, I have my peace of mind,
and in my ways, delight.
Though, perhaps, I should have listened more
to the words of Barry White...

Cushion

Whether you live in London,
or Liverpool, or Nepal,
there is only one cushion we have in this Life;
just one, and that is all.
Whether you were born in Boston,
or brought into the world in Bangkok;
whether or not you like liquorice,
or prefer easy listening to rock.
Whether the weather which suits your smile
occurs in autumn or spring;
whatever you wear, or your style of hair,
you can always be assured of one thing.
If you play gin rummy or poker;
or solitaire, blackjack, or whist;
you can bet your bottom dollar,
whether you stick or you twist,
that nothing can save us from ourselves,
if we should stumble, and fall.
the only cushion we have in this Life
is love...just love...and that's all.

A Tailor of Note

I bought a coat from a tailor of note;
who prided himself on his name.
It carried a label, which declared it able
to keep out the wind and the rain.
It was without hood, which wasn't so good,
but a hood didn't go with its style.
It fastened with ease,
and went down to the knees,
and the quality stood out a mile.
It was beigey-cream, if you know what I mean,
and double-breasted, to boot.
It kept me warm from dusk 'til dawn,
and fitted over my suit.
I wore the coat from the tailor of note
until it began to wear out.
Put to the test, it was past its best,
which was obvious, without any doubt!
So, I returned; for a new coat I yearned,
and I called on the tailor of note.
His shop wasn't there;
where it stood, all was bare;
I could hear the developers gloat.
His needle, his art, I now must impart
have fallen to progress and shame.
I once bought a coat from that tailor of note,
who prided himself on his name.

The Silent Ones

This is for the silent ones,
whose voice is never heard;
for the world is far too noisy,
to hear a whispered word.
And yet, they'd talk so easily,
if there was but an ear;
who'd listen without judgement,
and, by listening, hear.
Society has conditioned us
to listen with a view to reply.
Oh, that we could our quiet keep,
and stand supportively by.
Maybe then they'd open up,
and share their inner soul;
perhaps we'd have a picture
of how they tick, and roll!
So, this is for the silent ones,
who keep their thoughts inside;
who battle bravely, daily,
and all their feelings hide;
If we have the ears to hear,
and compassion, and empathy,
I'm sure that they would open up,
over a good cup of tea!

A Time for Grief

Sometimes, we're locked in grief so deep,
we cannot see for tears.
Our eyes are red with crying out
those words which no-one hears.
Our heads are bowed, our hearts are a weight
which is almost too heavy to bear.
Surely, there is nobody else
burdened with this care!
We cry to God, or to the moon,
to end our suffering now.
But, my dear, it is a passage of grief,
which we have to go through, somehow.
Loss is always painful,
It rips the soul apart.
It works its way into every chamber
of every broken heart.
And one day, when the sun comes out,
we'll slowly start to heal.
We'll hear the robin sing again;
we'll hear the church bells peal.
We'll find a purpose to our Lives,
when present pain is gone.
but 'til that day, let grief have its way;
'tis the strongest emotion, bar none.

Recipe for a Poet

Preparation time: As long as it takes.
(Cooking times vary, according to experience).

Serves: The World

Ingredients:

1 x Soul (any soul will do)
1 x Mind (open)
1 x Heart (broken)
1 x Pinch of wit
(you can always make that two).
1 x Sense of humour (essential)
1 x Cup of compassion
(to complement the heart)
1 x dessertspoon of humility.

Now you're ready to start!

Using the mind and soul as base,
take the broken heart.
Throw the pieces into the mix
and tear the lot apart.
When you've finished doing that,
it's time to let it heal.
That will take as long as it takes,
to make the poetry real.

Add a pinch of wit, or two,
to give the words some spark,
a sense of humour in everything,
stops the mixture becoming dark.
Add the compassion and humility.
Season with a little verve.
Now, you have a poet;
made, and ready to serve!

Addict

The Demon's in the drink,
and the Devil's in the dice,
The monkey's climbing up your back,
your senses to entice.
You know when you get that feeling,
it always ends the same.
The story of the addict,
and the placing of the blame.
A reason's never needed,
though many are often sought.
Lies are available, ready to hand,
lest red-handed, they be caught.
Nobody wants the world to know
they've spiralled out of control.
And so they try to hide it,
behind a fractured soul.
They exist inside their universe -
a tormented, solitary state,
where, drowning in their silence,
for their next fix, they wait.
Only they can break the circle.
Only they can change their way.
Only they can make a difference,
whatever people say.

If you're trapped inside the half-life,
and these words apply to you,
then only you can change the tune.
It's up to you to do.
For freedom waits on the other side
of whatever poisons your soul.
Take it from me, to reclaim your Life
is to score the winning goal.

Song of the Sailor

Where'er the wilful water runs,
that's where I'll make my home
I'll stand upon the shifting sands,
and gather grains in the gloam.
I'll pay the penance for my sins,
putting pennies in the pilot's hand.
For he will know I am of the sea;
and can no longer tarry on land.
I long to see white horses dance,
on the scent of the salty air;
and when the four winds blow, perchance,
I'll find my comfort there.
And so, I must set sail awhile;
my journey has begun.
The sea shall be my sweetheart;
my destiny, the sun.
For who could not contentment find,
when all is at one with the soul.
There is no place I'd rather be,
than where the billows roll.
Let my heart sing songs of joy!
To tawdry land - Goodbye!
My home is on the open sea,
'neath the ever-changing sky.

This is My Truth

I walk the walk of one whose worth
is measured by his own reasoning;
whose validation comes from the soul,
and whose inspiration is born from all around.
I have learned to accept, without craving
acceptance;
to give of myself, without giving in;
to dream, without dreaming my Life away;
and to follow my heart in its impetuosity.
I concern myself not with the days hence,
for they are the folly of imagination;
nor do I hunger for past glories
to light my footfall.
I walk this path alone in my skin,
and count my blessings as I find them.

Be Careful What You Tell Yourself

Be careful what you tell yourself,
in the smallest hours of the night;
it seems to matter so much more
than in the morning light.
It's what we allow ourselves to think
when sleep is far away,
which will determine how we rest,
and how we start our day.
If negative our musings be,
they'll put us in bad stead.
Not the best way to spend the time,
when you're lying awake in bed!
So tell yourself you're special;
that there's nobody else like you.
Count each one of your blessings;
I'll bet there are quite a few!
Tell yourself you're worth it;
make loving yourself a desire.
If you always want the best for yourself,
you'll find that your thoughts will be higher.
And please don't ever feel lonely,
when you're alone with your mind.
Everybody has something
which could make their back teeth grind!

It’s all down to what you tell yourself
by the glow of your bedside light.
So tell yourself you’re wonderful,
and I’ll bid you a fond goodnight!

Mountaineering

You'll never climb a mountain
if you give up on a hill.
Stop and rest, by all means;
but do not lose your will.
Some days you'll progress in leaps and bounds;
and forge magnificently ahead.
Others, you'll find you're on minimum drive,
and you'll struggle to get out of bed.
A rose never blooms all year round.
It's worth it to keep this in mind.
Some days are just for laying low,
and letting yourself unwind.
And on the days when strength has faltered,
with willpower in short supply,
be kind to yourself, and understand
that this will pass, by and by.
So keep on with your journey,
and all your dreams, fulfil.
You'll never climb a mountain,
if you give up on a hill!

Beauty

O! Lift that veil 'twixt good and ill!
For both are born in the mind.
Create the Life you want to Live!
Don't sit back so resigned!
Surround yourself with beauty!
Poetry is a start!
It leaps into the senses,
and stimulates the heart.
Follow that with music.
Be it sweet upon your ear.
Let it wrap around you,
and dance away your fear.
Let friends and family fill your soul;
for love makes this world go around.
Forget about things which you can't control,
and watch your blessings abound!
Take time to be alone with Nature.
Walk with her, hand in hand.
Be at one with being you;
don't be what others demand.
Add to all of this, candles;
To reflect the light in your eyes.
Find your peace in spite of your pain;
for that's where beauty lies.

Be You

Whatever you do today, be you.
Listen to your own soul -
not the opinions of others;
for they but see from their own level of
understanding.
The only acceptance and validation you need
comes from yourself.
If you seek power, then know who you are -
for that is the most powerful information you
can own.
Be content. Contentment outlasts happiness.
Whatever you do today, be passionate about it.
The world needs passion.
Don't half-be, or half-do anything. Give it your
everything,
whatever your endeavour.
Be slave to none, yet servant to all;
be there for their need, but not at their call.
Whatever you do today,
put your own stamp on it -
then you will have left something to be
remembered by.
Be adventurous; for adventure is what keeps the
child within alive.

Surround yourself with beauty, so that your
Life becomes enriched.
Count your blessings as you find them.
Be grateful for each moment, and learn from it.
But, most of all, my friend -
be you.

You're Not on Your Own

If, in silence, you could peep
into houses where other folk sleep,
you'd soon see tears, you'd soon see need;
and shattered dreams, and hearts that bleed;
a swinging door through which love has flown,
and stories similar to your own.
That is why I say, my friend,
what's happening now is not the end.
It's just a storm to weather out,
it's not what your whole Life is about.
This fleeting pain will disappear -
it may be tomorrow, it may be next year;
but eventually it will subside.
Peace will return at the turn of the tide.
So next time you think that no-one else feels
the grief you feel - remember, time heals;
And although your heart feels as heavy
as stone,
one thing's for certain - you're not on your own!

Before this Day is Over

Before this day is over,
let me give thanks for my lot.
Whatever has happened has happened.
Whatever is gone is forgot.
Let me not waste time complaining
about that which I cannot control.
Let me focus my mind on this moment;
and in it, nourish my soul.
For if I dwell upon the past,
or fear for what is to come,
I pay the price of present peace,
which is too costly a sum.
So may I savour each second,
and keep my dreams in sight;
before this day is over,
and I bid the world goodnight.

Don't Take it Personally

Don't take it personally,
or feel that it's your fault,
when someone dresses your wounds with salt.
It isn't your issue.
It isn't your call.
It's nothing to do with you;
nothing at all!
It's what's going on inside THEIR heads,
and whichever side they got out of their beds.
Maybe they've forgotten to take their meds,
or maybe they're just plain unhappy!
Whatever the reason,
let it go.
Be bigger than the situation.
Be thankful you're at peace with yourself,
and avoid an altercation.
For they're warring with themselves, in truth,
and are needing to vent their spleen.
The best thing you can do for yourself
is not get in between!
Keep your calm, and carry on,
and don't take them up on their ire.
There's no point in joining their battle,
and fighting fire with fire.

So, next time you're dodging bullets
from someone at odds with their mind,
remember to be understanding;
and, above all, don't be unkind.
You don't know what may have sparked them;
or what has caused their to-do!
Please! Don't take it personally!
That's my advice to you!

Blackpool

Should you ever visit Blackpool,
to take in the salt sea air,
there'll always be a welcome,
and a seagull, or two, waiting there.
Stretching along the Golden Mile,
are attractions by the score;
you can buy a portion of fish and chips,
candy-floss, rock, and more.
You can visit Madame Tussauds,
Ripley's 'Believe it or Not';
you can take in a show at the end of the pier,
in the summer, when the weather is hot.
If you're uncertain of your future,
and need clarification at all,
clairvoyants are dotted along the front,
watching Life through a crystal ball.
Should you prefer the fairground
as a place to get your kicks,
you can take a ride on The Big One,
or buy novelty walking sticks.
And when the autumn approaches,
the prom is the place to be.
You can see the Illuminations,
all lit up, for free.

So if you have a penchant
for the wearing of a hat;
you can invite the world to kiss you quick,
or take it further than that.
If you've never visited Blackpool,
it's worth the trip for a day.
An hour's drive up the M55,
if traffic doesn't get in your way.
You can tell I've a soft spot for Blackpool,
for it played a small part in my youth.
It suits me fine to revisit that time,
now that I am long in the tooth!
And so, I will remember
Blackpool, by the sea;
where, from the top of the Tower,
you can view infinity.

Dog Lovers

Dog lovers do in daylight.
They also do it at dark;
be it in a country lane,
or a municipal park.
They often stop for a natter,
like they've all the time on Earth.
Dog lovers have a secret,
and they know what that secret is worth.
No other folk are quite like them,
for you'll meet them in pouring rain.
If they were out without a dog,
you'd think them half-insane.
They always have treats in their pockets;
and black plastic bags in their hands.
They can often be heard muttering things,
which only their dog understands.
So here's to dog lovers everywhere;
for they are a breed apart.
It is the greatest joy in Life,
to have a dog in your heart!

On Reminiscing

So many tunes, so many rhymes;
so many memories, so many times.
Yet they are past, and gone away.
And all I'm left with is today.
Today's the day in which I Live.
I treat my memory like a sieve.
It holds the hearts of those who were dear,
but has no time for worry, or fear.
It also lets the bad slip through.
Why should I punish myself anew,
and face the failures of yesterday,
when only this moment is in play?
It's good, on occasion, to reminisce;
but heed my warning, and remember this.
For the time we are present here on Earth,
we should Live our Lives, for all they're worth!

Blips and Bleeps

Life is full of blips and bleeps,
though I don't know what they mean.
One says I have a message
appearing on the screen.
Another says my time is up,
and how much data I've used.
It's hardly any wonder
why I'm feeling so confused.
I only want to make a call,
and take the occasional snap,
All the rest of the paraphernalia
leaves me in a flap.
What happened to conversation -
the initial point of the phone?
I'm standing in a crowded room,
but ever so alone.
There are blips and bleeps going everywhere,
and everyone's face down.
What happened to eye contact?
What happened to looking around?
What happened to sweet silence
in which to gather a thought?
It's lost in a series of blips and bleeps.
Peace has come to nought.

So next time I hear a blip or a bleep
while I'm trying to relax,
I'll defenestrate the telephone.
Then, I'll be chilled to the max...

Fish and Chips

In England, Ireland, Scotland, and Wales,
there is a dish which never fails.
Guaranteed to bring delight,
it warms your insides on a stormy night.
It builds you up when you're on your knees,
and tastes even better with mushy peas.
Eat straight from the paper or use a plate,
either way, the taste is great.
Many make use of vinegar and salt,
though it's wise to know when to call a halt.
Some like to squeeze a dash of brown sauce,
or ketchup, if preferred, of course.
It doesn't matter how it's dressed,
as a filling meal, it's surely the best!
There's no better food to pass the lips
than a portion of good old fish and chips!

Cactus Jim

There was a man named Cactus Jim.
Have you ever heard of him?
I'm told that he lived way out west,
a-whittling on his porch in an old string vest;
drinking moonshine all day long;
playing his banjo, singing his song.
He could have been famous, Cactus Jim,
for the spiky hair which grew on his chin.
But he died alone on the prairie plain,
on a Sunday morning, when it started to rain.
It seems his liver wasn't too good,
and he hadn't thought, while whittling wood,
that all the drink he poured down his neck
would one day turn him into a wreck.
The moral of the tale is clear;
avoid the wine, the spirits, the beer;
or you could end up like Cactus Jim
(though no-one's ever heard of him...)

Dear Miss Frankenstein

Dear Miss Frankenstein,
your father is mad.
I'll bet he's up to mischief,
down there, in his pad.
Genetic engineering
is sort of where he's at;
he never comes up for dinner;
have you ever noticed that?
He's always busy when it's time for bed,
and he's still there in the morn;
a stranger man, Miss Frankenstein,
I swear has never been born.
Who knows what goings-on there are,
deep down in that cellar.
I can only assume, when he's in that room,
he's creating another fella.
And so, my dear Miss Frankenstein,
it only remains to say,
your father's as mad as a hatter;
I bid you a fond good day...

Don't Look Back in Rancour

Don't look back in rancour,
when reflecting on the past.
All has made you who you are,
and here you are, at last!
You've dealt with every day you've Lived -
each smile, each frown, each tear.
They've all been useful, in some way,
if you've learned from them, my dear!
Don't look back in rancour;
for it sours the present day.
Focus on this moment,
and what it has to say.
Experience is a teacher.
We learn, and then, we grow.
Regret is a wasteful option.
Release, and let it go.
Settle in the present.
Explore what it has to give.
Then, my dear, you can leave the past,
and truly start to Live!

Don't Be Afraid of the Dark

Don't be afraid of the dark, my dear.
Don't be afraid of the dark.
Light a candle to cheer your soul,
and imagination, spark.
Pick up a pen and find a blank page.
Write down what's held in your heart.
For that is where creativity's found,
so that is where you must start!
As candle burns, let mind run free.
Lose yourself in its flame.
O! But there's a comfort, there,
when Sadness calls your name.
Don't be afraid of the dark, my dear,
for that is when we shine.
Don't be afraid if your light is low;
please, bask awhile in mine.
For I have battled demons, my dear,
and wrested my soul from their hands.
I refuse to bow to their caprice
or give in to their demands.
Don't be afraid of the dark, my dear.
Don't be afraid of the dark.
Morning will come soon enough,
with the melody of the lark.

Until then, love the dark, my dear.
For it sings a different tune.
There's much to do, when day is done,
and we dance by the light of the moon.

The Letter

Sings the songbird, softly;
settling down to sleep.
I write a letter by the light of the lamp,
as evening shadows creep.
"To whom it may concern" it starts,
and carries on as thus...
"I want you to know you can change
your thoughts,
with the minimum of fuss.
When you start to drift into old routine,
and think of things that are gone;
or when you project your empty fears
onto what is to be later on...
you're forgetting about this moment -
for this moment is our lot!
We have no other time to Live,
to give it all we've got!
Tomorrow never happens.
Today is all time will allow.
Yesterday is over and done.
Better to Live in the now!"
And so, my friend, if you're reading this,
and you're wondering to whom it's addressed,
then let me put you at your ease,
and set your mind at rest.

It's written for the person
who needs to make time to 'be';
It certainly isn't aimed at you,
who thinks so mindfully!
It isn't for you, whose focus is clear;
who's aware of all that's around.
It isn't for you, who is living through
every sight and sound.
It's written to whom it may concern!
I composed it with love, and for free.
My dear friend, now you've read to the end,
I wrote the letter to me!

Fly

It's one o'clock in the morning;
there's the buzz of a fly in the room.
I should be in bed;
however, instead, I'm preparing for its doom.
It's kept me awake, for Heaven's sake,
for the past two painful hours.
My patience has been tested
(as have my swatting powers).
If it kept away from my face, okay;
I think I'd let it live.
But it keeps buzzing past
and it's much too fast,
and I'm too far gone to forgive.
It's not like we've formed an alliance.
Far from it. In fact, we're at war.
I've given it every chance to escape.
I've opened the windows and door.
What more does it need?
Will it ever concede?
My mind's at the end of its tether!
I wish that fly would buzz off, or die,
but I suppose it's expected, this weather.
An hour or so on, it still hasn't gone,
and my eyes have begun to turn red.

I'd give everything I have, at this point,
to settle down in my bed,
But I know I'll just lie awake, waiting.
Waiting, throughout the night,
for the fly to take its departure.
Until then, then I may as well write.
So here's a poem I've readily composed,
while time is passing by.
It is the tale of an epic fail
to rid my room of a fly.
So if you're as troubled as I am;
suffering, and under duress -
if it buzzes again,
take out paper and pen,
and have something to show for your stress...

Hoarders

Hoarders are a menace
to themselves and everyone.
There's always something on the floor,
which you can trip up on.
They also have 'Flat Surface Syndrome'
so there's nowhere to put things down.
You're stuck with holding your coffee cup,
whenever you go around.
There's all sorts of paraphernalia,
from everywhere they've been.
Bits and bobs, and odds and sods,
and all things in between!
On the mantelpiece is bric a brac -
it may be just junk to some -
but to the hoarder, it's treasure!
A memory of times long gone!
Hoarders never throw anything out,
in case they need it again.
They may have not needed it these last
twenty years,
But, hey! You never know when!
You may think I'm criticising -
but the opposite is true.
I'm on the side of the hoarders,
for I'm a hoarder, too!

Humans

Humans are strange creatures.
Here for a season,
we concern ourselves with
bills,
ills,
all sorts of pills,
battles of wills,
instant thrills,
and a television which fills the living room.
We spend our days in fear of dying.
In the meantime,
we forget to Live.

Hot Chocolate

I've taken to having hot chocolate,
before I retire to bed.
It's a far better soother than vodka,
and doesn't go straight to the head.
I wish I'd discovered it years ago,
to ensure a decent night's sleep,
instead of turning to alcohol,
and ending up in a heap.
For alcohol is a depressant;
it claws away at your dreams.
It's a fake and flaky friendship
which will rip you apart at the seams.
You'll lose your inhibitions.
You'll lose your self-respect, too;
and when it's taken all you have,
then, it'll come back for you.
So, if you're seeking a nightcap,
avoid the wine and the beer.
Never be tempted by spirits,
and away from caffeine, steer.
For all will have an adverse effect,
and you'll never get your eight hours;
but if you drink hot chocolate,
you'll be relaxed by its obvious powers.

It has the ability to comfort the soul,
when night-time rides into town.
You sip that silky liquid,
and swallow it slowly down.
All your troubles melt away,
and you feel a warmth within.
A mugful of hot chocolate,
is better than brandy or gin.
So when the darkness rolls around,
don't reach for the usual booze.
Make that mug of hot chocolate,
and put the world on snooze!

Idyll

Nobody's Life is an idyll,
whate'er they purport it to be.
Only here for a moment -
a speck in eternity...
Our heads and hearts are eaten up
by things beyond our control.
We allow ourselves to fall into
that all-consuming hole,
where everything we cannot do
becomes our driving force;
the faintest hint of the slightest breeze
blows us off our course.
And yet, if we our blessings count,
we can change our state of mind;
our journey may be lightened,
if we our purpose find.
For purpose is our reason,
to wake up each new morn;
It motivates us to the point
where inspiration's born
Seize the day with vigour;
and count your spiritual gold.
Your Life may not be an idyll,
but if you look, you'll find treasures untold!

Let Sleeping Dogs Lie

Let sleeping dogs lie.
Be not tempted to wake them,
lest, in fury, they fly!
Leave them peacefully musing on,
dreaming dreams of a bone.
Heed their gentle snoring,
and leave them well alone!
For who knows what goes around that brain,
when abed on home terrain!
What tales are in that reverie?
What thoughts do they entertain?
Are they replaying a game of ball,
or chasing a long-thrown stick?
Are they defeating their arch-enemies?
What makes those terriers tick?
By day, they're ever-playful.
They never stop for breath.
The most faithful of companions -
faithful unto death!
There is no welcome can compare;
no love, more honest and pure -
than that of a devoted animal
whose heart is steadfast and sure.
And yet, I give a warning
which is not to be taken light.
Always let a sleeping dog lie,
for if you wake him, he may bite!

Lionel

"O! Lend me your shoulder, Lionel!"
said the Lady of the House.
"I think I may be fainting;
for I've just seen a mouse.
Lionel, be a darling;
and help me onto a chair!
I don't want a mouse running up my leg,
and into my underwear!"
Lionel, being lovely,
lifted her into the air.
Now Lionel and the Lady are married,
because a mouse started off the affair.
The moral of the story is simple;
Great things from tiny things grow.
like giant oaks from acorns;
like blood drops on the snow.
One never knows the moment
when opportunity comes to call.
Therefore, be you watchful for mice,
and other things just as small...

Of Palaces and Prisons

The mind comes as an unfurnished room,
full of nothing, but thoughts.
'Tis we who give it fabric,
and a substance, of sorts.
A palace or a prison?
Choose your decor well!
How we perceive our surroundings,
puts us in Heaven or Hell.
If we furnish it with fear of folk,
and what they think or say,
we're as good as shackled in our cell,
the key being thrown away.
To break free from this wretched pen,
where opinions make up your bed,
simply remove the need to explain,
and create some space in your head!
Fill it, then, with music,
and poetry for the soul.
Do not allow another's hand
to exercise control!
You'll never know contentment,
if, to others' whims, you bow!
Furnish your mind with beauty,
and build your palace, now!

On Eccentricity

'Eccentric' means 'out of centre' -
not wishing to conform.
To fall in line with everybody else,
is certainly not their norm!
They have the curiosity
belonging to a child;
though, from the outside looking in,
we'd think them a little wild!
They're certainly individual,
and cannot be defined.
They have the most original thoughts
occupying their minds!
They dress that wee bit differently,
to suit their current mood.
They're usually highly intelligent,
and with a sense of wit are imbued.
Strongly idealistic,
their beliefs are set in stone.
They never fall in with others' opinions,
as they're way out there on their own!
So, if you know an eccentric,
treasure them like gold,
for they are few and far between,
these people who bare their souls.

They Live Life on another plane,
where beauty is their lot.
The thing about eccentrics is
they'll never be forgot!!!

On Soul Searching

We fill ourselves with lovers,
and stuff ourselves with cake.
We hide our pain from others,
and all diversions take.
We'd tame a thousand lions;
and trek to the North Pole -
rather than sit in silence,
and question our own soul.
Because that means evaluation
of who we are, and why.
What is it, then, that irks us,
when we look ourselves in the eye?
Is there something in that mirror
telling truths we don't want to hear?
Will it take too much effort, this journey?
Is it laziness, or fear?
Whatever it is, we're losing out,
if we don't explore who we are.
We'll never learn about ourselves,
if we don't want to travel that far.
For journeys are their own reward;
they change the way we think.
Each step brings knowledge, and wisdom.
From the fountain of us, let us drink!

The Unforgiven

Please forgive the unforgiven,
for they know not what they do.
And while you're at it, forgive yourself;
for you're on that list, too!

Past Historic

If ever I fell beneath a spell,
and was forced to tell the truth;
I would honestly say I'd rather today,
than those heady days of youth!
No teenage angst to deal with;
no falling foul of a fight;
no romance to excite my day,
or keep me from sleep at night.
There is no point in looking back
for I follow my heart, all the way.
I've made enough mistakes to know
no peace lies in yesterday.
A healthy knowledge of self and soul
has grown from those little seeds.
I no longer look to the ways of the world
to fulfil my wants and needs.
So when someone wishes they could go back
to live it all again,
I remind them that they can do this,
if they pick up a paper and pen!
For when we write, we Live Life twice,
so embrace your current time.
Experience teaches everything;
gold from the deepest mine!

We are not slaves to memories,
which feed upon our fears.
Remember the past, by all means;
but don't let it kill you, my dears!
Remember the past, by all means;
but don't let it kill you, my dears...

Plastic Wrapping

Plastic wrapping is anathema.
The end of the World is nigh.
It's wrapped around virtually everything;
everything you buy.
And what a nightmare to open!!!
You end up using a knife,
to slice right down the crease of it.
Slip, and you could lose your Life!
And still the thing is tightly bound;
I scratch my nail across;
But all I do is scar it.
Now I'm really at a loss.
I've even tried it with my teeth,
But all to no avail.
The gift I'm struggling to open,
is still in its plastic jail.
One day, there'll be an invention,
to whip off this accursed stuff.
In the meantime I'll just sweat it out,
and sit and huff and puff.
And when my tether is at its end,
and the plastic is firmly stuck.
I'll hand it over to someone else;
and see if they have any luck...

The Wisdom of Trees

I tarried awhile in shady glen,
in the bosom of the trees.
Cradled in their countenance,
I sank down to my knees.
A silent prayer was on my lips,
a fever on my brow.
I sought the solace of yesteryear,
dismissing the gift of now.
I fell asleep where I had lain,
and dreamed of days gone by.
Therein, I found no answer,
for time does nothing but fly.
But in that quiet moment
'twixt sanity and space,
I realised yesterday was gone;
this moment was in its place.
My reverie was broken,
by the sound of leaves on the breeze.
I stood with my eyes open,
and listened to the wisdom of trees.

A Matter of Life and Death

Death is but a part of Life;
as much a part as birth.
In the time between, we should celebrate
the hours we spend on Earth.
For bodies age, and then break down;
the rickety frame gives way.
There comes a time, when all of us
must leave this madcap play!
So awaken your sense of adventure!
Set off from your comfort zone!
Leave that land of lethargy!
Leave it well alone!
Grasp each opportunity;
hold it in both hands!
Follow your dreams, wherever they lead;
and do as your soul commands!
For what is Life but this moment?
What purpose are we to fulfil?
My dear, when that is revealed to you,
you'll have no more hours left to kill.
No more endless boredom,
wishing your week away.
Shine your Light, Brave Candle!
Give meaning to your day!

For when the evening shadows fall,
and our homeward way we wend -
Look back, but not in anger,
when day is at its end.

Poet

Live your Life as a poet,
though words, be not your strength;
Life should be measured by its fullness,
no matter what its length.
A poet sees beauty in the shape of a stone,
and finds comfort in the bosom of the night.
There is no fear of time spent alone,
by the softness of candlelight.
For inspiration is everywhere
the poet cares to look.
the creative mind will find fantasy,
in every cranny and nook.
The feel of wet grass on freezing feet,
the cold morning rain on the face;
The chirp of the robin from a chestnut tree,
the poet's soul can embrace.
The scent of gardenia on the evening air,
the honeysuckle hailing the bee.
the sight of a swallow at summers start;
all arouse serenity.
So Live your Life as a poet,
and wake up to wonder each day.
Never let the ticking clock
tick your Life away.

Be present in Life's presence,
and Live it to the full.
If you Live it as a poet,
no moment will ever be dull!

Roar

O! where the quiet mountain,
where I can roar, untamed?
Unlike Whitman's own barbaric yawp,
my sound shall remain unnamed.
For it will soar to the heavens,
and increase, as higher it climbs.
It will not fail, or falter,
or fall to paltry rhymes.
It will hide its loss of innocence,
as it calls out to the wild;
for though I am my own hero,
I still have the heart of a child.
And yet, there is a sound in me,
matured through pain and tears;
though I care not now for what went before,
for naught can change those years.
And so I roar of acceptance,
and pray that my voice may be heard;
for acceptance has been my redemption;
that, and enlightening word.
Both have shaped the sound of my roar,
into what it is today;
though we cannot escape experience,
we can learn along the way.

And so, I beg you, whatever your roar -
whatever has brought you here -
Let the world in wonder stand,
as you sound out, loud and clear!
We all can be our own heroes,
as bandaged and bruised, we ride on.
Cast off each thought of tomorrows.
Let your heart and your voice be as one.
Embrace this very moment;
for now is all that we own.
So find your quiet mountain,
and let your roar be known!

Seize the Day

Like seconds, our hours rush by,
unnoticed,
as we hurtle from birth to death.
We tread well-worn paths,
which have become slippery
under the soles of willing walkers,
sliding into oblivion
as they clutch their security blankets
close to their chests.
Hampered by their chains,
they drop their dreams down drains,
until all that remains is frustration
at fear of failure, and feeling unfulfilled.
Break the mould. Forget the old.
Hold onto those dreams.
Never give your soul away!
Carpe Diem! Seize the Day!

STOP! DIVERT!

On days when Life is an uphill struggle,
and patience starts to fray;
when obstacles the size of trees
are put into my way,
I remind myself of its transience -
this trampoline state of mind.
Nothing is of permanence.
All can be redefined.
So, by changing the negative thought,
and thinking 'STOP! DIVERT!' -
I replace it with a moment of beauty,
to soothe away the hurt.
I count my every blessing,
and give thanks for them all.
I stop, and name them, one by one,
as each one I recall.
The list of blessings grows each day
that I, the effort make.
'Be' in every moment -
nothing's a mistake.
It's all part of the learning curve -
this journey of humankind.
Stay in the now! Don't fear what's ahead!
And NEVER look behind!

The 'F' Word

I fondly, and foolishly, fell in love
with a fanciful femme fatale.
She forged her fetters around my heart,
that faithless, flighty gal.
For fine was I, and fair was she,
and foggy was the night.
She found herself a firefighter,
whose flame she could ignite.
Our affair finished there, at the foot of the stair,
as the stars from the firmament fell.
They came to rest upon the blessed -
those lovers who never know hell.
"O! Fie!" said I, to folk nearby,
not desiring to further the fuss.
I fastened my tie, and tried not to cry;
and that was the end of us.

On the Passing of a Mother

Without pomp, or circumstance,
we laid you down;
scattering earth on hallowed ground.
We talked of times long-gone before,
when you would greet us at your door,
with a welcome word and a cheery smile -
and some good advice -
that was so your style.
But now we say our last goodbye,
and bid farewell with heavy sigh
to all that was, but is no more...
to your sweet spirit, gone before.
In our hearts you shall remain,
and on our tongues will be your name.
Though Life must leave us, by and by,
your memory will never die.

The Flower Seller

I saw a solitary flower seller
standing on the street.
She'd blooms of every strain and hue;
her hair was short, and sweet.
In alto voice, she sang a song,
which filled the morning air.
I was wont to listen;
and so, I tarried there.
What rapturous melody it was!
What haunting highs she hit!
And though she sang but to herself,
'twas joyous! I admit!
Yet no-one stopped to buy her wares,
or listen to her song.
She sang, like a nightingale alone,
distanced from the throng.
O! Save us from indifference!
From rushing through the day!
From missing opportunities,
whenever they come our way!
If we our Lives with beauty fill;
then Life is not a chore.
It is a grand adventure,
delivered to our door.

So, next time the traveller in you stirs,
and you desire to venture abroad,'
listen for the air of a song on the breeze;
as a nightingale's soul is outpoured!

The Man in the Shed

Surely you must have heard, or read,
all about the man in the shed?
He potters around, the whole day long,
fixing things which have somehow gone wrong;
a nail for this - a screw for that,
some binding for a cricket bat -
a spot of glue, to hold a shoe,
(a bit of tape, it's as good as new).
There are umpteen jars on umpteen shelves;
(we may say it's excessive, between ourselves)
but in each jar there's just the right bit -
he knows that only one will fit.
It's no use using a two-inch nail
for a three-inch hole. That's bound to fail!
But for the sake of careful thought,
all his deeds would come to nought.
However, the day is invariably saved,
as he is to bits and bobs enslaved.
In the drawer, he keeps his rasps and files;
on the floor there are left-over quarry tiles.
It's like a little home from home;
with his radio on, he's never alone.

He's at his happiest when totally engrossed,
sipping his tea, and munching on toast,
the worries of the world he lets slip by,
as he ponders on providence,
and stars in the sky.
I'm an awful lot like the man in the shed,
but my passion is tinkering with words,
instead!

The Old Days

What was it like in the old days, Dad,
when people wore flares,
and good times were had?
What were the songs that floated your boat,
while you posed in Virgin, in your Afghan coat,
listening to your favourite tunes,
after buying a new pair of loons?
What was it like at the Stadium gigs,
drinking Heineken lager, smoking No.6 cigs?
Did you buy anything from Antwacky's Bazaar?
Did you have a Columbus or Jedson guitar?
And were you the coolest dude on the street -
a splash of Brut, and platforms on feet?
Playing your tunes through a Sound City amp -
Holding down barre chords which
gave you cramp.
Dodging skinheads on the last bus home;
hoping that they would leave you alone,
But secretly knowing that you if you
looked around,
They'd be in for a penny and in for a pound,
And you'd be chased right up the street,
and you with your platforms on your feet.
It occurs to me, you must have been mad.
So what was it like in the old days, Dad?

The Smile

He kept his dream in a cardboard box,
to be opened, once in a while.
In it, wrapped in innocence,
was a wide-eyed, small boy's smile.
He'd forgotten how to wear it,
what with life, and choices, and all.
But he needed to look, every now and then;
whenever he felt withdrawal.
He needed to look to make sure it was there;
that it hadn't faded away;
for if it at all were possible,
he'd wear it again, one day...
one day when the leaves were green,
and the stars, in alignment, fell;
one when he would wake up,
and everything would gel.
He knew that day would never come,
for chance is an ungainly beast.
It lumbers into our consciousness,
on our souls to feast.
So, never hide your dream in a box,
to be opened, once in a while.
Set it free, and follow it;
and you'll surely find your smile!

Age is Nothing at All

When you think of the fun you've had
when young,
age is nothing at all.
Getting ready on a Saturday night
to go out and have a ball!
Music blasting from speakers;
no wonder you struggle to hear!
But that was how it was, back then;
year, after year, after year!
When you count the kisses on your cheek,
age is nothing at all.
On days when times seem cold and bleak,
close your eyes and recall.
Every memory is Life well-lived;
for to Live is why we are here!
Don't put things off 'til tomorrow -
next week, next month, next year!
When you smile at the wisdom which you
have acquired,
age is nothing at all.
You leave well alone those things you
can't change,
rather than foolishly fall.
Never wish to be young again,
when now you sleep soundly at night.
Memories are dreams which are past and gone.
If you want to re-live them, then write!

The Personal Touch

What's missing today is the personal touch.
When people answered phones, and such,
you knew that someone was on the case;
and you had contentment on your face.
Now, you're passed from pillar to post.
You speak to someone, but it could be a ghost;
as you're left on hold for an hour or more,
staring into space, or gazing at the floor;
listening to tunes which fry your brain,
as they come back and ask you again for
your name.
Then you have to press 1 or 2,
only to find that you're tenth in the queue.
Days can pass before it comes to your turn;
you've atrophied, and all life adjourned,
while whoever it is on the other end
(if they're not asleep, Heaven forfend...)
has probably gone off to make a drink,
leaving you with nothing but time to think.
I much preferred a friendly voice,
not a recorded message with multiple choice.
Take me back! It's not asking much!
I miss the days of the personal touch!

The Poet's Art

To the mind of a poet,
nothing is mundane.
The cogs are always turning,
in that effervescent brain.
Poets dance with their naked souls,
their passion to ignite.
When words are failing all around,
the poet starts to write!
And in their words we find a balm
to ease our hurt and pain.
Our suffering is reflected;
our emotions are the same.
Our innermost thoughts are exposed to all;
reflected in a verse.
It is as though the poet knows
what makes us tick, and worse!
And yet, we bathe in the comfort
that we are not alone.
We compare the poet's state of mind
with that of our own.
And grateful are we that someone's words
can mollify the heart;
For to write what we cannot say -
that is the poet's art!

A Dream Unopened

I found a dream, unopened;
boxed, with its seal intact.
It was lying, quite abandoned;
gathering dust, in fact.
I wouldn't presume to take it,
but it gave me a moment's pause;
and I mused who it could have belonged to.
I wonder, now...
was it yours?

The Prodigal Sock

My story's not told to frighten or shock,
'tis merely the tale of the prodigal sock...
one which vanished months ago;
when the fields were hard and covered in snow.
I'd put it safely in the washing machine,
and from that moment on,
it has never been seen.
Its partner lingered, lonely, and blue,
along with paired socks, of every hue.
Each time I opened the wooden drawer,
I could see it in the corner...
I'd searched the floor.
I'd looked in every cranny and nook,
no hiding place did I overlook.
And then, this morning, to my surprise,
there it was, before my eyes;
the prodigal sock, with its dark blue stripes,
jammed behind the radiator pipes!
I freed it from its secret lair,
and now I have back my favourite pair.
The moral here is pretty clear.
Never worry, never fear.

Perhaps you've said goodbye to your dream,
or lost it in the washing machine.
Maybe it's hung on some forgotten line,
waiting, just, waiting, for you to find.
Please, sit you down, and take good stock;
and remember the tale of the prodigal sock!

When Somebody Close Returns Again Home

When somebody close returns again home,
and we are left to mourn;
let us not in anger grieve -
although our hearts be torn.
Let us rejoice in their memory.
and smile at the sound of their name.
May it not fill us with anguish;
may it not wrack us with pain.
For they have Lived their time on Earth;
and now, that time is done.
The next part of their journey
has only just begun.
So let us give thanks for their teaching;
for we learn from each other, it's true.
And in that way, we have been blessed,
by the love of the person we knew.
We'll miss their physical presence;
of that, there is no doubt.
We'll miss the sound of their familiar voice.
We'll miss seeing them about.
Yet, they Live on all around us;
everywhere we look.
They are found in forest flowers,
and in each shady nook.

They're in each feather falling,
and in the robin's song;
the butterflies of summer
on angel wings come along.
They're never far from where we are;
they're only a thought away.
And they'll keep watching over us,
'til we return home, one day.

The Sandman's Pocket

In the Sandman's pocket,
is the ticket to a dream.
The price is what you can afford,
when you've run out of steam.
A wish is what you ask for,
to turn this world about.
Close your eyes, and count to ten.
Whisper. Please don't shout.
The Sandman hears you well enough,
for his ear is as big as his heart.
Settle down inside his arms,
and all of your cares, impart.
In return, you will learn
there is much you can achieve;
the moment you stop doubting,
and in miracles, believe!
In this world of dreamtime,
the oppressor's hand is stayed.
The arrogant are brought to bear.
The powers that be are afraid.
Fallen are the mighty.
The weak become the strong.
The children, lost in wonder,
sing their usual song.
And I, a child in spirit,
am happy to sing along.

When the Curtain Comes Down

Where do we go when the curtain comes down?
To a restaurant? Or a party?
Or a new club in town?
What do we do when the audience goes home,
and the ghosts of the theatre are wont to roam?
Perchance we talk of old times past,
and share a laugh with the rest of the cast.
Or maybe we go to our digs, alone,
looking forward to the phone call home.
How do we feel at the end of the play,
when silence replaces the lines that we say?
Whether we be actor, singer, or clown,
we all wonder what awaits us, when the curtain
comes down.

The Stingwell Down

As I approached the Stingwell Down,
that lonely field of odd renown,
my eyes upon a stranger fell,
who would the strangest story tell.
He'd set up camp, the previous night,
and ate his supper by firelight.
Settling down with a cup of tea,
and a bowl of soup for company,
he heard a sound from the neighbouring wood -
a sound which truly curdled his blood.
A shriek, like a banshee's,
howled through the trees;
the temperature dropped by significant degrees,
and he, being frozen to the spot,
shape or form, he could see not;
but again he heard the terrible shriek;
closer now – a breath on his cheek...
A voice from nowhere, calling out;
Calling for help, there is no doubt!
As darkness fell o'er the Stingwell Down –
that lonely field of odd renown;
I swear I heard someone calling my name,
and looked to see from whence it came.

Yet, when I turned, the man had gone;
No trace of a fire, or anyone...
O! Now I think I am going insane!
There! Again! I hear my name!!!
O! To be in my bed asleep,
than on this field with my flesh a-creep.
I wish I'd not come to this lonely moor,
alive with spirits gone before.
I turn to run, but trip on a stone.
No longer now, am I alone.
The long-dead face of a circus clown
meets my gaze, on the Stingwell Down.
They found my body the following day.
All the papers seemed to say
was that I had given in to fright;
my face contorted, in the morning light.
Reader, do not tarry around,
if you're ever near the Stingwell Down.
For the spirits of those who've gone before
will welcome you in through the open door.
Never think it won't happen to you,
for I'll be there, to greet you too...

The Trolley with a Mind of its Own

I took my tiny token, and put it in the slot.
A quick dash around the supermarket
was to be my lot.
I didn't have much time to spare,
and only a few things to buy;
I'd made myself a shopping list,
so around the place, I'd fly.
At first I thought the lock had jammed,
as the trolley wouldn't pull out.
It had taken several bashings,
and the wheels were up the spout.
Nonetheless, I soldiered on;
and eventually reached the door.
I tried to guide it smoothly,
across the supermarket floor.
But it was having none of it;
the thing was fighting back.
I attempted to manoeuvre past the veg,
and hit the Easter egg stack.
Down the eggs came, one and all,
I ignored them and pushed on ahead.
I aimed it at the apples,
but it swerved toward a woman instead.

I apologised profusely,
as it bumped into her beam.
She turned, and gave me a frosty glare,
wanting to let off steam.
I hurried down the middle aisle,
The thing was all awry;
I managed a full one-eighty,
to avoid being left high and dry.
I dragged it behind me ‘til I reached the till,
and unloaded it onto the belt.
I couldn’t wait to bag my stuff,
that’s how frustrated I felt.
I finally emerged into open air,
and, eventually, made my way home;
hoping I never encounter again
the trolley with a mind of its own.

To One in Disarray

I said to someone, yesterday,
who phoned last night, in disarray,
to say that someone was rocking their boat.
"Don't give them the power" I said, and I quote.
Nobody has power over you,
until you give power away.
You have your very own force shield,
so bring that shield into play.
Let their words bounce off into nothingness,
and don't take their anger on board.
Observe, by all means, but don't absorb;
that way, calm is restored.
For calm, and peace, should be our goals;
no other gifts are so rare!
If we can hold them to our breasts,
and carry them everywhere,
we have the blueprint for Living Life -
the definitive design!
So, dear friend in disarray -
Hark these words of mine!

Reflections on the Day

When sat in reflection on the day,
and the air has a melancholy lay;
let not your soul be troubled, I say;
though, with head in hands, you weep.

When all feels hopeless, and all seems lost;
and the price of a memory is whatever it cost;
and your heart's like a cauldron, but your brain
is like frost,
the hill you climb is steep.

Keep on! Keep on! Keep keeping on,
until the road you travel's done.
The day may have been lost or won;
but put it, now, to sleep...

For we shall never see it more.
It has, like a dancer, left the floor;
no bouquet of flowers, no sweet encore,
We sow, and so we reap.

Farewell, farewell, then, to the dying light.
When you wake in the morning, as stars take
flight,
may you find yourself with countenance bright,
and at each opportunity, leap!

To Quieten the Anxious Heart

Surround yourself with silence.
Face your fears head on.
Breathe in slowly, and deeply.
Breathe out what's past and gone.
Have no concern for tomorrow;
for today holds cares of its own.
Allow each thought to come, and pass.
Don't dwell on it, alone.
Do not write scenarios
before the truth be heard;
and never hang your answer
on an unsaid word.
Be positive in your thinking,
and to the facts adhere.
Continue to breathe in deeply;
and quieten that heart, my dear!

Today Will Be a Good Day

Today will be a good day.
This, I understand;
(nothing to do with the weather)
and all, as yet, unplanned.
Today will be a day of note;
I aim to make it so.
Negativity shall not call,
as onward and upward I go.
I won't give in to worry;
for worry does no good.
It saps the strength from a sturdy soul
and dampens the fire in the blood.
Today will be a good day,
be it filled with sun or rain;
therefore, I will meet it
without the need to complain.
Each precious second I will use
to make a better me.
I'll stay within the moment,
and set my spirit free!
Today will be a good day,
though my path be strewn with stones.
Today will be a good day!
I feel it in my bones!

Too Great a Mind

Be of too great a mind to concern yourself with
the affairs of others.
Be of too bright a mind to allow the darkness to
cloak your shine.
Be of too adventurous a mind to tether yourself
to old thinking.
Be of too hungry a mind to starve yourself of
opportunities.
Be of too brave a mind to not face up to yourself.
Be of too determined a mind to let obstacles
stand in your way.
Be of too open a mind to harbour
narrow opinions.
Be of too curious a mind to stop learning,
of too fertile a mind to stop growing,
and of too beautiful a mind to fret your
Life away!

Vestige

I howl your name to the hollow night,
for in that void is no delight.
I write to scratch the itch away,
so let the words come, come what may.
For poetry is oft inspired
by a mantle of sorrow, when the mind is tired.
The heart remembers what it chooses to forget,
Time is the healer. We heal, and yet...
there is always a vestige to hang dreams upon.
though past is over, and done, and gone.
And so I let memories pass on their way,
for they have no more that they want to say.
I smile, and recover, for this moment is all.
And in it, I'll dwell, whate'er should befall!

The Days When Vinyl was King

I danced with every beat of my heart,
in the days when vinyl was king.
I even made some records myself,
though they didn't do a thing!
But I was part of an era,
when you had the sleeve notes to read.
They weren't tiny words on a CD cover,
where two lines in, you concede.
You walked from the shop with a tangible thing,
when you purchased a brand new LP.
You couldn't wait to get it back home,
to give it a spin or three.
When the needle went down on side one of
the disc,
and you heard the static sound,
you knew you'd soon be in vinyl heaven,
with your earphones wrapped around.
Your parents didn't get it at all,
though my Dad loved the Moody Blues.
(He was right when he said "You'll damage
your feet,
going out in those pointy-toed shoes").
I remember the thrill of my first kiss.
I thought my soul would sing!
I also remember the tears I cried,
in the days when vinyl was king.

But that was growing up back then,
though a Lifetime ago it now seems!
We Lived the soundtrack to our Lives;
the music fostered our dreams.
And now those crackly old records,
hold memories in their grooves.
I may not be able to dance these days,
but I still remember the moves!
Alas, there's too much looking back!
To the past we should never cling!
But I can't help having a soft spot,
for the days when vinyl was king.

Vive la Difference

If everybody dared to be different,
what a dazzling world this would be;
if people didn't care so much,
what other people see!
If everybody dared to be different -
by being who they really are -
maybe this Earth would heal itself
without so much as a scar.
Yet, cloister'd do we keep our thoughts,
and we dress as we do every day.
We try not to attract attention,
so we keep our heads down, all the way.
O! For the courage to just be ourselves!
What a change in our Lives we would see!
We'd happily take no notice
of those who would have us unfree.
We wouldn't give a tinker's cuss
about what people think.
It wouldn't matter the tiniest jot,
we wouldn't even blink!
I pray we all wake up one morn,
with a spring in our step as we stroll;
and a little voice of confidence
telling all "THAT'S HOW I ROLL!!!"

Waiting for the Weekend

I waited for the weekend,
but all it did was rain;
so I hung my hat on Monday,
but Tuesday got into my brain.
On Wednesday, I was full of woe,
wishing I'd stayed in bed.
Only Thursday and Friday to get through...
should Friday go ahead.
Which takes me to the weekend,
and the ever-present rain.
I've wished a week of my Life away.
Now, isn't that insane!!!

Byron Most

There was a man called Byron Most;
who lived in a cottage on the south-west coast.
Each morning he'd take the seaside air,
as he walked the prom with style, and flair;
past the tideline of rusting hulls,
avoiding the eyeline of pigeons and gulls.
Dapper was the man, for sure;
his obvious charisma, and natural allure
shone from his iridescent soul,
whenever he set out to stroll.
He'd wave to folk as he went on his way,
and always passed the time of day.
He seemingly didn't have a care,
at least, if he did, no-one knew it was there.
And so it was, with great surprise
(as it often is when someone dies)
that we received the terrible news;
he'd left no letter. He'd left no clues,
as to why he'd chosen to leave this earth;
He was big on smiles, yet low on mirth;
and nobody thought to ask how he was;
he always seemed fine, and that was because
he hid his pain in a deep, dark place,
and always put on his happy face.

What a shame we didn't know;
his loss has been a terrible blow.
Perhaps, in future, we should be
more open with our company;
and never be so self-engrossed
that we fail to see people like Byron Most.

What is a Poem

What is a poem?
Is it just a collection of thoughts,
randomly written down,
without care for form or rhyme?
Or is it something more cohesive?
Something scribbled in rhythm and time?
Does it have to be hard to understand,
and carry a secret theme?
Or should it be inspirational...
and raise your self-esteem?
Does
        it
           drop
               you
          like
      an
arrow
and make a valid point?
Isitcleverinitsquirkiness?
Does it your soul anoint?
Should it comfort a broken heart,
or should it raise a smile?

It doesn't matter what you write,
as long as you do it with style!
Let your words come from deep within.
Let your mind 'round the Universe roam!
Then, my friend, take out paper and pen,
and hey presto! You'll have written a poem!

What People Think

Worry not what people think!
They all have fears of their own!
Release yourself from that prison!
Let go of that heavy stone!
Be you, in all your glory!
Step out there in style!
Don't hide away in your darkness,
searching for your smile.
If folk don't like you as you are,
that's their issue, not yours!
If you live for their approval,
you'll die, without their applause!
So worry not what people think.
Their 'opinion' doesn't count!
Don't let them sway you from your path;
not by the slightest amount!
To thine own self be true, as Shakespeare said.
Understanding is knowing yourself.
If people are powerless over you,
then, my friend, you have great wealth!
I pray you use that wealth wisely,
and give it to those in need!
Spread the word to help the others,
who others' opinions heed!

Wildflowers

I walk in contentment, where wildflowers grow
and hold their heads up high.
Far away from the straight and the narrow,
they smile toward the sky.
They need not careful pruning.
They are as nature meant;
flourishing in their habitat;
delicate, their scent.
They care not to be careful
to be in shade or sun;
they spring up in their fashion,
until their days are done.
And so I walk among wildflowers,
all the livelong day.
For they grow far from the concrete path,
in wonderful display.
They cheer the heart, and feed the soul,
falling easy on the eye.
Let me Live my Life among wildflowers,
until the day I die!

Beatitude

I live alone,
but I'm never lonely.
I have a phone,
and my house is homely.
There are memories
from over the years;
some bring laughter,
some bring tears.
I have wonderful friends,
and food on my plate.
My trials are many,
but my blessings are great.

Arabian Eyes

In a part of Asia Minor,
where Life could not be finer...
I gave my heart to a Turkish girl,
in lipstick and eye-liner.
She didn't want to see the world,
or sail the seven seas.
She was happy to stay at home,
with the sunshine and the breeze.
For on that Anatolian coast,
who could want for more?
Fresh sea-bass would do that lass,
whose beauty was hard to ignore.
She had no wish for other fish,
for she only dined on the best;
that vision with Arabian eyes,
and an Ottoman heart in her breast.
I wonder what became of her,
not that I need to know,
for many summers and winters have passed,
and it was so long ago.
Ah, memories, which take me back
to my time in Asia Minor.
I wouldn't have missed the experience,
for all the tea in China.

Words

Words...
In sequence they fall.
Sometimes, they mean everything;
sometimes, nothing at all.
Sometimes, they take forever
to get from A to B;
but, their sweet meanderings
are treasury to me!
They light the shadow'd path ahead,
and dance upon the page;
they leap from my untidy mind,
and demand the centre stage.
O rare communication!
O where the sting of death,
when wise bon mots are utter'd,
with someone's final breath?
Words shall be my medium;
my offspring, and my delight.
By morning they are seeded,
and come to fruition at night.
And so I shall my pen allow
to run as free as my heart;
for wherever words await me,
there lies my fractur'd art!

All the World's a Stage

All the world's a stage, my dear.
All the world's a stage.
Each living thing will sing its song,
save the bird inside its cage.
For it knows no taste of freedom,
and cannot swoop and dive.
Joy is not within its heart
to truly feel alive.
All the world's a stage, my dear.
All the world's a stage.
If courage be our watchword,
then hearts we must engage.
For Life is too soon over,
and all the parts we play
will one day be forgotten,
along with the lines we say.
All the world's a stage, my dear.
All the worlds a stage.
Therefore, be you truthful,
whatever years your age.
Grow within your chosen sphere,
and fill your own blank page.
All the world's a stage, my dear.
All the world's a stage.